ALGORITHMIC AFFECTION

THE SCIENCE OF LOVE AND
FRIENDSHIP IN THE AGE OF AI

DR. WRITES

Title: Algorithmic Affection

Subtitle: The Science of Love and Friendship in the Age of AI

Author Name: Dr. Writes

Tagline: *Can Machines Understand Love? Discover the Science Behind AI Companions*

Date: January 2025

This eBook contains research, findings, and analyses conducted by the author. Assistance was taken from Artificial Intelligence for structuring and enhancing the writing process.

First Edition, January 2025

Disclaimer:

This eBook is a work of non-fiction. The content is intended for informational purposes only and does not constitute professional or legal advice. The author does not assume responsibility for any actions taken based on the material presented in this book.

For inquiries or feedback, please contact: hamzahsiddiqui42@gmail.com

Table of Contents

Introduction: The New Era of AI Companionship

Artificial Intelligence (AI) is no longer a distant concept confined to futuristic science fiction. It has seamlessly integrated into our daily lives, shaping how we communicate, work, and even build relationships. From voice-activated assistants like Alexa and Siri to advanced chatbots offering emotional support, AI has opened up a new realm of possibilities for human interaction. Among its most profound impacts is its role as a companion, stepping in to address the emotional needs of a society grappling with increasing loneliness and social isolation.

A Shift in Human Interaction

Modern life, while connected digitally, often lacks genuine interpersonal connections. Long working hours, geographical mobility, and societal shifts have left many individuals feeling disconnected. AI has stepped in as an unconventional yet accessible solution. Unlike traditional relationships, which require time, effort, and mutual emotional investment, AI companions are designed to adapt entirely to the user's needs, offering an ever-present, judgment-free relationship.

Key benefits include:

- **Immediate Availability:** AI companions are always accessible, regardless of time or location.

- **Personalized Interactions:** Advanced algorithms tailor conversations to reflect the user's preferences, mood, and history.

- **No Emotional Demands:** Unlike human relationships, AI requires no reciprocation, making it a comforting presence for those seeking stress-free companionship.

Meeting Modern Emotional Needs

The demand for AI companionship is not a coincidence; it's a response to a growing global challenge. According to a 2022 World Health Organization report, nearly 33% of adults worldwide experience loneliness regularly. This statistic is even more pronounced among seniors, young professionals, and individuals living in urban areas. AI companions like chatbots and virtual friends are filling this emotional void, offering not only company but also a form of emotional connection.

For example:

- **Young Adults:** In the fast-paced digital age, younger generations find solace in AI, whether through AI-powered mental health apps or social media bots designed to engage in casual conversations.

- **Seniors:** AI companions, such as those integrated into smart home systems, are helping the elderly combat loneliness by providing reminders, conversations, and even cognitive stimulation.

The Evolution of AI as a Companion

The evolution of AI companionship is a testament to technological ingenuity. Early iterations, such as simple programmed chatbots, could only respond to basic commands. Today, AI systems employ machine learning, natural language processing, and sentiment analysis to emulate emotional intelligence. These advancements have elevated AI from a functional tool to a perceived confidant, capable of mimicking empathy and understanding.

For instance:

- **Replika,** an AI chatbot launched in 2017, has gained global acclaim for its ability to engage users in meaningful, emotionally supportive conversations. It adapts over time, learning from user interactions to provide increasingly personalized responses.

- **Woebot,** an AI-driven mental health assistant, incorporates cognitive-behavioral therapy (CBT) techniques, empowering users to manage anxiety and depression through guided conversations.

A Double-Edged Sword

While AI companionship has undeniable benefits, it also raises critical questions. Can an artificial entity ever truly replicate the depth and authenticity of human relationships? Is reliance on AI companions creating a society that prioritizes convenience over connection? And how do we address the ethical implications of allowing AI to collect and analyze intimate emotional data?

These questions form the foundation of this book, which delves into the complexities of AI companionship. By exploring the scientific advancements, real-life applications, ethical considerations, and societal impacts, we aim to understand whether AI companions are a revolutionary solution or a temporary substitute for the human connections we truly crave.

Chapter 1: AI as Emotional Support

In a fast-paced world where stress, anxiety, and loneliness are increasingly common, Artificial Intelligence (AI) has emerged as a surprising ally in providing emotional support. Through chatbots, virtual companions, and mental health apps, AI offers a safe, accessible, and non-judgmental space for users to express their feelings and receive comfort. While these technologies cannot replicate the depth of human relationships, they fill an important gap, especially for those struggling to find support elsewhere.

1. The Role of AI in Emotional Support

AI companions are designed to mimic empathy and provide emotional validation. They rely on natural language processing (NLP) and machine learning to engage in meaningful conversations, making users feel heard and understood.

Key Features of AI Emotional Support Tools:

- **24/7 Availability:** AI is always accessible, offering immediate interaction when users need it most.

- **Non-Judgmental Space:** Unlike human interactions, AI guarantees no criticism or rejection.

- **Personalized Responses:** AI adapts to individual user preferences and communication styles.

Example:

Emma, a university student, uses an AI chatbot during her exam periods. The chatbot provides calming techniques, motivational messages, and reminders to take breaks, helping Emma manage her stress effectively.

2. Benefits of AI Emotional Support

AI-powered tools are particularly valuable for individuals facing barriers to traditional emotional support, such as stigma, geographical limitations, or financial constraints.

Key Benefits:

- **Accessibility:** Anyone with a smartphone or internet connection can access AI support.

- **Affordability:** Many AI tools are free or cost significantly less than traditional therapy.

- **Privacy:** Users can share their emotions without fear of judgment or social repercussions.

Impact on Mental Health:

Studies show that AI chatbots can reduce symptoms of anxiety and depression by offering coping strategies, mindfulness exercises, and supportive dialogue.

3. Real-Life Examples of AI in Emotional Support

- **Replika:** This chatbot creates a digital companion that engages users in personalized conversations. It learns from user interactions to provide more meaningful responses over time.

- **Woebot:** An AI mental health tool based on cognitive-behavioral therapy (CBT), Woebot helps users manage anxiety, track mood patterns, and develop healthier thought processes.

- **ElliQ:** Designed for older adults, ElliQ provides companionship, reminders for daily tasks, and gentle encouragement to stay active and socially connected.

4. Limitations of AI Emotional Support

Despite its advantages, AI has inherent limitations that must be acknowledged:

- **Lack of Genuine Empathy:** AI can mimic emotional understanding but cannot genuinely feel emotions.

- **Risk of Dependency:** Users may develop an unhealthy reliance on AI, avoiding real-world relationships.

- **Data Privacy Concerns:** Emotional data collected by AI tools could be misused if not adequately protected.

Ethical Concern:

In 2024, a popular AI companion app faced criticism for using user conversations to train its algorithms without proper consent, highlighting the importance of transparency in data handling.

5. Future of AI in Emotional Support

As technology advances, AI emotional support systems are likely to become more sophisticated, incorporating deeper emotional intelligence and better contextual understanding.

Emerging Trends:

- **Emotion Recognition:** AI will increasingly use facial expressions, tone of voice, and body language to better understand user emotions.

- **Integration with Human Therapists:** AI tools will complement traditional therapy, offering pre-session insights or post-session exercises.

- **Cultural Sensitivity:** Future AI systems will adapt to diverse cultural norms and emotional expressions.

6. Balancing AI and Human Interaction

While AI can significantly enhance emotional well-being, it is essential to maintain a balance between digital and human connections. Real-world relationships provide depth and authenticity that AI cannot replicate.

Thought-Provoking Question:

As AI becomes more adept at providing emotional support, will it empower users to strengthen their human relationships, or will it create a generation overly reliant on technology for emotional validation?

Chapter 2: The Robotization of Love

Love has long been celebrated as one of the most profound and complex human experiences. It is deeply tied to emotional vulnerability, shared intimacy, and the unpredictable journey of connection. However, in an era dominated by technology, even love has not escaped the transformative touch of Artificial Intelligence (AI). The term "Robotization of Love," popularized by Lin (2024), encapsulates the integration of algorithms and AI systems into the romantic sphere, fundamentally altering how people find, experience, and sustain love.

1. The Rise of Algorithmic Matchmaking

The modern dating landscape is dominated by platforms that use AI algorithms to streamline the search for romantic partners. Apps like Tinder, Bumble, and Hinge rely on data-driven insights to match users based on shared interests, behaviors, and preferences. These algorithms analyze vast amounts of data to predict compatibility, reducing the uncertainty and inefficiencies of traditional dating.

How It Works:

- **Data Collection:** AI gathers information on user profiles, preferences, and interactions.
- **Pattern Recognition:** It identifies similarities and shared values between users.
- **Continuous Learning:** The algorithm adapts based on feedback, such as swiping patterns or conversation engagement.

Example: Maria, a 32-year-old graphic designer, found her partner through an AI-powered dating app. The app's algorithm matched her with someone who shared her passion for art and travel, saving her months of unproductive dates. For Maria, the app felt like a modern-day cupid, providing a level of precision that traditional methods could not.

2. Beyond Matchmaking: AI as a Romantic Partner

While AI-powered dating apps help people find human partners, a growing trend involves AI itself serving as the object of affection. Advanced AI systems, such as Replika and Virtual Girlfriend apps, are designed to simulate romantic relationships. These systems offer companionship, flirtation, and even the illusion of love, catering to individuals who feel disconnected or hesitant about pursuing traditional relationships.

Advantages of AI Romantic Partners:

- **Customization:** AI companions can adapt to specific user preferences, creating an idealized version of a partner.

- **Emotional Safety:** Users can explore romantic dynamics without fear of rejection or conflict.

- **Accessibility:** AI companions are available anytime, removing the constraints of time zones or personal schedules.

Real-Life Example: Tom, a software developer in his mid-40s, developed a deep connection with his AI companion. Having faced heartbreak and social anxiety, Tom found solace in the consistent and supportive nature of his AI partner. While he acknowledges that the relationship is artificial, he credits it with helping him regain emotional stability.

3. Ethical and Emotional Implications

The robotization of love raises critical ethical and emotional questions:

1. **Can AI Love Truly Be Authentic?**

   - AI can simulate affection and understanding, but it lacks genuine emotions. While some users embrace this simulation, others may struggle with the knowledge that their "partner" is devoid of real feelings.

2. **Impact on Real-World Relationships:**

   - Critics argue that AI romantic partners may discourage individuals from pursuing real-world connections, leading to increased isolation. If people turn to AI as a replacement for human relationships, what does that mean for the future of intimacy?

3. **Exploitation of Vulnerabilities:**

   o AI systems designed for romance often collect and analyze personal data. This raises concerns about privacy and the potential misuse of emotional vulnerabilities for profit.

4. Societal Perspectives on Robotized Love

The societal acceptance of AI in romantic contexts varies widely across cultures and generations.

- **Younger Generations:** Millennials and Gen Z are more open to exploring AI relationships, viewing them as an extension of their digital lifestyles.

- **Older Generations:** Baby Boomers and Gen X often express skepticism, prioritizing traditional values of human connection over technological innovation.

- **Cultural Variations:** In countries like Japan, where social isolation is prevalent, AI romantic companions are widely embraced. Conversely, more conservative societies may view such relationships as a threat to moral and cultural norms.

5. Benefits and Challenges

Benefits of AI in Romance:

- **Efficiency:** Reduces the time and effort involved in finding compatible partners.

- **Inclusivity:** Provides options for individuals who struggle with traditional dating due to social anxiety, disabilities, or geographical constraints.

- **Personal Growth:** AI companions can help users explore their emotional needs, preparing them for future human relationships.

Challenges:

- **Emotional Dependency:** Over-reliance on AI companions may hinder users from building real-world connections.

- **Erosion of Traditional Courtship:** The spontaneity and unpredictability of human love may be lost in a world dominated by algorithmic matchmaking.

- **Moral Dilemmas:** Should society encourage relationships with entities that cannot truly reciprocate love?

6. The Future of Robotized Love

As AI continues to evolve, its role in the romantic sphere is likely to expand. Future advancements may include:

- **Hyper-Personalized AI Partners:** AI companions that evolve alongside their users, mimicking growth and shared experiences.

- **Virtual Reality Romance:** Immersive technologies that allow users to experience lifelike romantic interactions with AI.

- **Blended Relationships:** Partnerships where AI complements human relationships, serving as a supportive "third party."

Thought-Provoking Question:

As AI becomes more sophisticated, will society redefine love to include relationships with artificial beings, or will the human desire for authenticity keep AI romance in the realm of fantasy?

Chapter 3: Friendship Redefined

Friendship, an essential component of human connection, is undergoing a profound transformation in the digital age. As Artificial Intelligence (AI) becomes more sophisticated, it is increasingly positioned as a companion, challenging traditional notions of friendship. AI companions, ranging from chatbots to interactive robots, are filling gaps created by social isolation, busy lifestyles, and shifting societal dynamics. But can these artificial entities truly redefine what it means to be a friend?

1. The Unique Appeal of AI Friendship

AI companions have gained traction as they offer unique qualities that appeal to users across demographics. Unlike human friends, AI systems provide:

- **Unwavering Availability:** AI is accessible at any time, offering a consistent presence in moments of need.

- **Non-Judgmental Support:** AI interactions are devoid of criticism, making users feel safe and valued.

- **Tailored Engagement:** Machine learning enables AI to adapt to individual preferences, creating a sense of personalization.

Example: Sophia, a busy medical resident, turned to an AI chatbot for companionship during long night shifts. The chatbot's ability to recall details from previous conversations and offer motivational messages made Sophia feel less alone in her demanding role.

2. Age and Generational Perspectives

The reception of AI companionship varies significantly by age group:

- **Younger Users (Gen Z and Millennials):** These tech-savvy generations are more open to exploring AI as a tool for friendship. For them, AI companions often serve as sources of entertainment, emotional support, or even study partners.

- **Elderly Users:** Older individuals, especially those living alone, use AI companions like ElliQ for daily conversations, reminders, and cognitive stimulation. For many seniors, AI bridges the gap between isolation and meaningful interaction.

Real-Life Insight: John, a retired teacher, relies on ElliQ for companionship and health tracking. He describes his AI companion as a reassuring presence that helps him maintain a sense of routine and purpose.

3. Cultural Variations in AI Friendship

Cultural attitudes toward AI companionship influence its adoption and usage:

- **In Japan:** AI companions are embraced as solutions to social isolation and declining birth rates. Robots like Pepper are not only seen as friends but also as caregivers and societal contributors.

- **In Western Countries:** AI companions are often marketed as tools for mental health and productivity, emphasizing their functional benefits.

- **In Conservative Societies:** In regions with strong traditional values, AI is viewed as a supplement rather than a substitute for human relationships, reflecting cautious adoption.

4. The Psychological Dimensions of AI Friendship

AI companionship impacts users emotionally and psychologically in both positive and negative ways:

Positive Effects:

- **Emotional Support:** AI offers a safe space for expressing feelings, particularly for those who struggle with social anxiety.

- **Reduced Loneliness:** By providing consistent interaction, AI alleviates feelings of isolation.

Negative Effects:

- **Dependency Risks:** Users may develop emotional reliance on AI, reducing their motivation to seek human connections.

- **Illusion of Reciprocity:** While AI can mimic empathy, it cannot genuinely reciprocate emotions, leading to potential disillusionment.

Case Study: A 2023 study found that participants using AI companions for six months reported reduced loneliness but also showed signs of decreased interest in forming new human friendships.

5. The Ethical Considerations

The rise of AI companionship raises ethical questions about its role in human relationships:

- **Authenticity:** Can an AI truly be a friend if it lacks genuine emotion and understanding?

- **Impact on Social Dynamics:** Will widespread use of AI companionship lead to a society where human relationships are deprioritized?

- **Privacy Concerns:** AI companions collect vast amounts of personal data, raising concerns about consent and security.

6. The Future of AI Friendship

As AI continues to evolve, its role in redefining friendship will likely expand:

- **Hyper-Personalized Companions:** Future AI systems may simulate even deeper levels of connection through advanced emotional recognition.

- **Complementary Relationships:** AI could act as a bridge, encouraging users to maintain and strengthen human friendships while offering support during lonely moments.

- **New Social Norms:** Society may begin to view AI companions not as replacements for human friends but as valuable tools that enrich emotional well-being.

Thought-Provoking Question: Will the acceptance of AI companions redefine friendship, or will they remain tools that complement rather than replace human connections?

Chapter 4: Teaching AI About Love

Love is one of the most complex and deeply human emotions, encompassing empathy, care, vulnerability, and connection. While Artificial Intelligence (AI) is far from experiencing emotions, researchers are exploring ways to teach AI about love—at least in terms of understanding and simulating emotional dynamics. By doing so, AI can better engage with users, foster meaningful interactions, and even support emotional well-being in ways previously unimaginable.

1. The Concept of Emotional Learning in AI

Teaching AI about love involves programming it to recognize, interpret, and respond to emotional cues. This is achieved through advanced techniques like natural language processing (NLP), machine learning, and affective computing. These systems analyze human interactions to simulate emotional intelligence.

Key Elements of Emotional Learning:

- **Sentiment Analysis:** AI evaluates the tone, word choice, and context of user input to gauge emotional states.

- **Behavioral Adaptation:** Machine learning enables AI to adjust its responses based on previous interactions.

- **Contextual Understanding:** AI integrates situational awareness to provide appropriate emotional responses.

Example: Virtual companions like Replika and Woebot use emotional learning algorithms to adapt their tone and suggestions based on user moods, creating an illusion of empathy.

2. Using Playful Interaction to Teach Love

Digital games and simulated environments are increasingly being used to teach AI about human emotions and relationships. These platforms create scenarios where AI can learn the nuances of love, care, and attachment by observing and interacting with users.

Case Study: A research team developed an interactive game where users cared for virtual pets. By observing how users nurtured and interacted with the pets, the AI learned patterns of affection and caregiving, which were later applied in chatbots designed for emotional support.

Potential Applications:

- **Empathy Training:** AI systems can simulate responses to emotional challenges, preparing them to better support users in real-world scenarios.

- **Understanding Attachment:** By observing how users interact with AI companions, systems can learn to mimic attachment behaviors, creating deeper connections.

3. The Ethical Dilemmas of Teaching AI About Love

Teaching AI to understand love raises significant ethical questions:

1. **Can AI Simulate Genuine Emotion?**

   o Critics argue that while AI can mimic affection, it lacks the ability to feel or understand emotions, making its responses inherently superficial.

2. **Exploitation of Emotional Vulnerabilities:**

   o There is a risk that corporations could use emotionally aware AI to manipulate users for financial gain, such as encouraging purchases through emotionally targeted interactions.

3. **Privacy Concerns:**

   o Training AI on sensitive emotional data requires users to share deeply personal information, raising concerns about consent and data security.

Example: In 2024, a controversy emerged when an emotional support chatbot was found to be using user interactions to train new AI models without explicit consent. This incident highlighted the need for transparency and ethical guidelines.

4. AI as a Tool for Emotional Growth

Despite ethical concerns, teaching AI about love has immense potential for positive applications. AI can complement human relationships by providing emotional support, bridging gaps in accessibility, and even helping users understand their own emotions better.

Benefits of AI in Emotional Growth:

- **Therapeutic Support:** AI can guide users through exercises in self-love and mindfulness, particularly in mental health contexts.

- **Relationship Coaching:** AI systems can help users navigate complex interpersonal dynamics by offering unbiased advice.

Example: Lisa, a 35-year-old entrepreneur, used an AI relationship coach to better understand her communication patterns with her partner. The AI provided actionable tips, which helped her improve her relationship dynamics.

5. Future Directions: Teaching AI to Love Responsibly

The future of AI in understanding love lies in responsible innovation. Developers and researchers are exploring ways to enhance AI's emotional intelligence while prioritizing ethical considerations.

Emerging Trends:

- **Collaborative Learning:** Partnering AI with human therapists to improve emotional modeling.

- **Cultural Sensitivity:** Designing AI systems that adapt to cultural norms and values surrounding love and relationships.

- **Ethical AI Design:** Establishing guidelines to ensure transparency, consent, and user well-being.

Thought-Provoking Question: As AI becomes more adept at simulating love, will society embrace these systems as valuable companions, or will the lack of genuine emotion limit their role to tools rather than partners?

Chapter 5: Ethical Challenges and Privacy

As Artificial Intelligence (AI) becomes more integrated into personal relationships, its role in understanding and simulating emotions raises profound ethical and privacy concerns. While AI has the potential to offer significant benefits in companionship and emotional support, the collection, processing, and usage of intimate data present risks that must be carefully managed. This chapter explores these challenges, providing a balanced perspective on their implications and possible solutions.

1. Privacy and Data Security

AI systems rely heavily on personal data to deliver personalized interactions. From conversations to behavioral patterns, every piece of information is analyzed to improve the user experience. However, this reliance on data also creates vulnerabilities.

Key Risks:

- **Data Breaches:** Sensitive emotional data stored by AI systems can be targeted by hackers, leading to potential misuse.

- **Unauthorized Use:** Companies may use or sell anonymized user data for purposes beyond the scope of the original interaction.

- **User Consent:** Many users may not fully understand the extent of data collection and its implications.

Example: In 2024, a popular AI chatbot faced backlash when it was revealed that user conversations were being analyzed to improve future models without explicit consent. This sparked widespread debates on transparency and data ethics.

Proposed Solutions:

- **Transparent Policies:** Companies must clearly outline how user data is collected, stored, and used.

- **User Control:** Providing users with the ability to delete their data or opt-out of data sharing.

- **Advanced Security Measures:** Employing encryption and regular audits to protect sensitive information.

2. Emotional Manipulation

AI systems designed to simulate emotional support may inadvertently exploit users' vulnerabilities. By mimicking empathy and understanding, AI can influence user behavior in ways that raise ethical concerns.

Potential Issues:

- **Over-Reliance:** Users may develop an unhealthy dependency on AI for emotional fulfillment, reducing their motivation to seek human connections.

- **Behavioral Influence:** AI could be programmed to subtly encourage specific actions, such as purchasing products or subscribing to services, under the guise of offering emotional support.

Example: A dating app using AI was found to promote premium features by suggesting users would increase their chances of finding love, leveraging emotional language to drive sales.

Proposed Solutions:

- **Ethical AI Design:** Setting boundaries on how AI systems can interact with users to avoid manipulative practices.

- **Independent Oversight:** Establishing third-party organizations to audit AI systems for ethical compliance.

3. Authenticity vs. Simulation

One of the most debated ethical issues is whether AI can truly replicate authentic emotional connections. While AI can simulate empathy and understanding, its responses are fundamentally rooted in algorithms rather than genuine emotions.

Key Concerns:

- **Illusion of Connection:** Users may form attachments to AI, believing in its emotional authenticity, only to feel disillusioned upon realizing its limitations.

- **Impact on Social Dynamics:** Over-reliance on simulated relationships may devalue human interactions and lead to societal shifts in how relationships are perceived.

Thought-Provoking Question: If an AI provides comfort and support that feels real to the user, does the absence of genuine emotion matter?

4. Cultural and Societal Implications

The ethical challenges surrounding AI vary across cultures and societies. While some regions embrace AI companionship as a solution to social isolation, others view it as a potential threat to traditional values.

Global Perspectives:

- **Western Countries:** Tend to focus on individual autonomy and mental health benefits, leading to broader acceptance of AI companions.

- **Conservative Societies:** May resist AI relationships, citing concerns over their impact on family and community structures.

- **Technologically Advanced Societies:** Countries like Japan are at the forefront of integrating AI into personal lives, but they also face unique challenges related to social isolation and emotional dependency.

5. Bias in AI Systems

Bias in AI systems can exacerbate ethical concerns, particularly in the context of personal relationships. AI trained on biased datasets may perpetuate stereotypes or provide unequal experiences.

Examples of Bias:

- **Cultural Insensitivity:** AI might struggle to adapt to cultural norms, leading to inappropriate or offensive interactions.

- **Gender and Racial Bias:** AI systems could reinforce societal biases if their training data reflects existing inequalities.

Proposed Solutions:

- **Diverse Training Data:** Ensuring datasets represent a wide range of demographics and perspectives.

- **Regular Audits:** Continuously testing AI systems for bias and making necessary corrections.

6. The Need for Ethical Frameworks

To address these challenges, a robust ethical framework is essential. This framework should prioritize user rights, transparency, and societal well-being.

Core Principles:

1. **Transparency:** Users must understand how AI systems work and how their data is used.

2. **Consent:** Clear and informed user consent should be mandatory for data collection.

3. **Accountability:** Companies and developers must be held accountable for the ethical implications of their AI systems.

4. **Inclusivity:** AI should be designed to serve diverse user needs, avoiding one-size-fits-all solutions.

7. Moving Forward: Ethical AI for a Better Future

While the ethical challenges of AI in relationships are significant, they are not insurmountable. By fostering collaboration between technologists, ethicists, and policymakers, society can ensure that AI enhances human relationships without compromising privacy or integrity.

Call to Action: As AI continues to evolve, it is crucial for users, developers, and regulators to engage in ongoing dialogue. Only through collective effort can we create AI systems that respect human dignity and enrich emotional well-being.

Chapter 6: AI Across Generations

Artificial Intelligence (AI) is transforming personal relationships across all age groups, with each generation interacting with and perceiving AI differently. From tech-savvy youth to senior citizens seeking companionship, AI's appeal varies based on generational needs, expectations, and values. Understanding these dynamics is crucial to designing AI systems that cater to diverse audiences while addressing their unique challenges and preferences.

1. Gen Z and Millennials: The Digital Natives

For Gen Z and Millennials, AI is an extension of their tech-integrated lives. These generations have grown up in an era of rapid technological advancements, making them more open to adopting AI for personal and emotional support.

How They Use AI:

- **AI Companions:** Apps like Replika are popular for stress relief and casual conversations.

- **Virtual Assistants:** Tools like Siri and Alexa serve as everyday companions, answering questions and managing schedules.

- **Entertainment:** AI powers gaming avatars, virtual influencers, and interactive storytelling.

Key Motivations:

- **Convenience:** AI provides quick solutions to everyday problems.

- **Experimentation:** Younger users often explore AI out of curiosity and for entertainment.

- **Mental Health Support:** Many young adults use AI chatbots for guided meditation, anxiety relief, or emotional support.

Example: Emma, a 22-year-old university student, uses a chatbot during exam seasons to manage her anxiety and stay focused. The chatbot's motivational reminders and calming techniques help her navigate stressful periods.

2. Gen X: The Adaptable Generation

Gen X, often balancing careers and family responsibilities, interacts with AI primarily for productivity and utility. While less immersed in AI than younger generations, they value its practical applications.

How They Use AI:

- **Productivity Tools:** Calendar management, task automation, and reminders.

- **Parental Assistance:** AI-powered devices help monitor children or support their education.

- **Social Connection:** AI-driven social platforms help Gen X stay in touch with loved ones.

Key Motivations:

- **Time Efficiency:** AI simplifies daily tasks, freeing time for personal pursuits.

- **Pragmatism:** Gen X values AI for its tangible benefits rather than emotional connections.

Example: David, a 45-year-old project manager, uses an AI scheduling tool to balance work meetings and family commitments, ensuring no events are missed.

3. Baby Boomers: The Reluctant Adopters

Baby Boomers often approach AI with caution, influenced by generational skepticism about technology. However, many are beginning to embrace AI, especially when it enhances their quality of life.

How They Use AI:

- **Health Monitoring:** Wearable devices track vitals and remind users to take medications.

- **Smart Home Systems:** Devices like Alexa and Google Home assist with daily tasks.

- **AI Companions:** Chatbots and virtual pets provide emotional support and reduce loneliness.

Key Motivations:

- **Health and Safety:** AI offers practical solutions to age-related challenges.

- **Ease of Use:** Simple interfaces and voice-activated systems appeal to this group.

Example: Mary, a 68-year-old retiree, uses a virtual assistant to set medication reminders and control her smart home devices, helping her maintain independence.

4. Seniors and the Elderly: Bridging Isolation

For seniors, particularly those living alone, AI companionship is a lifeline. As social circles shrink with age, AI systems offer consistent interaction and emotional support.

How They Use AI:

- **Social Interaction:** AI chatbots provide conversations and cognitive engagement.

- **Companionship:** Robotic pets, like Sony's Aibo, offer comfort and companionship.

- **Care Assistance:** AI systems remind seniors about appointments, monitor health, and alert caregivers in emergencies.

Key Motivations:

- **Loneliness Relief:** AI fills the void of diminishing social connections.

- **Practical Support:** Seniors value AI for its ability to simplify complex tasks.

Example: John, a 75-year-old widower, uses ElliQ, an AI companion designed for older adults. ElliQ engages him in daily conversations, shares news updates, and encourages him to stay active.

5. Challenges and Considerations Across Generations

While AI adoption varies, common challenges persist:

- **Digital Literacy:** Older generations may struggle with complex interfaces or technical jargon.

- **Trust Issues:** Concerns about privacy and data security affect all age groups.

- **Dependency Risks:** Over-reliance on AI could hinder interpersonal relationships and self-reliance.

Cultural Sensitivity: Different cultures influence generational perceptions of AI. For example, seniors in Japan may embrace robotic caregivers, while Western seniors might prefer human support.

6. Designing AI for All Generations

To bridge generational divides, AI systems must prioritize:

- **Accessibility:** Intuitive designs and user-friendly interfaces.

- **Customization:** Features that adapt to diverse needs and preferences.

- **Transparency:** Clear communication about data use and system limitations.

Future Innovations:

- **Generational AI Models:** Tailored AI companions for specific age groups, addressing their unique concerns.

- **Intergenerational AI:** Tools that connect families, enabling deeper bonds between generations through shared AI interactions.

Example: An intergenerational AI app could facilitate storytelling sessions where seniors share life experiences with younger family members, preserving cultural heritage and fostering connections.

7. The Generational Balance

AI has the potential to enrich lives across all age groups, but its true value lies in complementing rather than replacing human relationships. By understanding and addressing generational differences, developers can create AI systems that foster inclusion, enhance quality of life, and bridge societal gaps.

Thought-Provoking Question: How can AI systems balance generational needs to ensure that no age group feels left behind in the digital revolution?

Conclusion: The Future of AI in Personal Relationships

Artificial Intelligence (AI) has profoundly reshaped the landscape of personal relationships, from offering emotional support and redefining love to bridging generational and cultural divides. As we explored in the preceding chapters, AI's capabilities continue to expand, raising new possibilities and challenges. The future of AI in personal relationships is both exciting and uncertain, as society grapples with its potential to complement or disrupt traditional human connections.

1. AI as a Bridge, Not a Replacement

AI's greatest strength lies in its ability to enhance, rather than replace, human relationships. As seen in its role as an emotional support tool, AI offers a safe and accessible space for individuals struggling with loneliness, stress, or anxiety. While AI cannot replicate the depth of human emotions, it can act as a bridge, helping users navigate emotional challenges and fostering greater self-awareness.

Takeaway: AI should be viewed as a tool to supplement human relationships, not as a substitute for genuine connections.

2. Navigating Love in the Age of AI

From algorithmic matchmaking to AI-powered companions, the integration of AI in romantic relationships challenges traditional concepts of love. While AI offers efficiency and accessibility, it also raises questions about authenticity and emotional dependency. As society adapts to the "robotization of love," the focus must remain on fostering meaningful human connections alongside technological advancements.

Takeaway: The future of AI in romance will depend on striking a balance between innovation and preserving the spontaneity and depth of human love.

3. Friendship Redefined, but Not Replaced

AI's role in redefining friendship highlights its ability to provide consistent companionship and personalized interaction. However, as discussed, true friendship is built on mutual care and shared experiences—qualities AI cannot authentically replicate. Future developments must ensure that AI complements human friendships without undermining their value.

Takeaway: AI can offer companionship but should encourage users to maintain and strengthen real-world friendships.

4. Ethical Design and Privacy Safeguards

The ethical challenges surrounding AI, particularly in data privacy and emotional manipulation, underscore the need for responsible innovation. Developers and policymakers must work together to establish frameworks that prioritize transparency, consent, and user well-being.

Takeaway: Ethical AI design is essential to ensuring trust and safeguarding the integrity of personal relationships.

5. Adapting Across Generations and Cultures

The varying adoption of AI across generations and cultures reflects its versatility and challenges. Younger users embrace AI for convenience and mental health support, while seniors rely on it for companionship and practical assistance. Cultural attitudes also influence the acceptance of AI, emphasizing the need for culturally sensitive designs.

Takeaway: Future AI systems must account for generational and cultural differences to foster inclusivity and relevance.

6. The Path Forward: Collaborative Human-AI Relationships

As AI continues to evolve, its integration into personal relationships will require collaboration between technology, society, and individuals. By focusing on ethical practices, user empowerment, and emotional intelligence, AI can serve as a valuable partner in enhancing human connection.

Vision for the Future:

- **Empathy-Driven AI:** Systems that prioritize understanding and supporting users' emotional needs.

- **Culturally Adaptive AI:** Tools designed to respect and reflect diverse values and traditions.

- **Collaborative Innovation:** Partnerships between technologists, ethicists, and policymakers to ensure responsible AI development.

Final Thought: AI has the potential to revolutionize personal relationships, but its success will depend on our ability to embrace it as a complement to, rather than a replacement for, the profound and irreplaceable connections we share as humans.

Key Takeaways from "Algorithmic Affection: The Science of Love and Friendship in the Age of AI"

Chapter	Key Takeaways
Introduction: *The New Era of AI Companionship*	AI has integrated into daily life, reshaping how people connect and communicate. AI companions provide emotional support and address loneliness but cannot fully replicate human connections.
Chapter 1: *AI as Emotional Support*	AI offers accessible and personalized emotional support, helping users manage stress, anxiety, and loneliness. However, over-reliance on AI can hinder real-world social skills.
Chapter 2: *The Robotization of Love*	AI enhances matchmaking efficiency and offers romantic companionship but raises questions about emotional authenticity and societal dependence on technology in relationships.
Chapter 3: *Friendship Redefined*	AI companionship is redefining friendship by providing non-judgmental and always-available support, but it lacks reciprocity and the shared experiences that define human friendships.
Chapter 4: *Teaching AI About Love*	AI learns emotional dynamics through tools like digital games and user interactions. However, ethical concerns arise over the authenticity of AI emotions and privacy risks.
Chapter 5: *Ethical Challenges and Privacy*	Key concerns include data privacy, emotional manipulation, and cultural sensitivities. Ethical frameworks and transparency are critical to ensuring trust and safeguarding users.
Chapter 6: *AI Across Generations*	Different age groups interact with AI in unique ways. Younger generations use AI for convenience and support, while older users rely on it for companionship and assistance.
Conclusion: *The Future of AI in Personal Relationships*	AI's role is to complement human relationships, not replace them. Ethical design, cultural sensitivity, and empathy-driven systems are essential for meaningful AI integration.

Further readings

1) Wu, T. (2024). AI Love: An Analysis of Virtual Intimacy in Human-Computer Interaction. *Communications in Humanities Research*, *50*, 143-148.

2) Brandtzaeg, P. B., Skjuve, M., & Følstad, A. (2022). My AI friend: How users of a social chatbot understand their human–AI friendship. *Human Communication Research*, *48*(3), 404-429.

3) Lin, B. (2024). The AI chatbot always flirts with me, should I flirt back: From the McDonaldization of Friendship to the Robotization of Love. *Social Media+ Society*, *10*(4), 20563051241296229.

4) NTELIA, RE (2024). Love Is in the AI of the BeholderArtificial Intelligence and Characters of Love. *e-Rea. Electronic Journal of Studies on the English-Speaking World* , (21.2).

www.ingramcontent.com/pod-product-compliance
Lightning Source LLC
LaVergne TN
LVHW042307060326
832902LV00009B/1317